Reg 29503

11.50

WITHDRAWN

Diary of a
MOTOCROSS
Freak

Heinemann
LIBRARY

www.heinemann.co.uk/library
Visit our website to find out more information about **Heinemann Library** books.

To order:
☎ Phone 44 (0) 1865 888066
📄 Send a fax to 44 (0) 1865 314091
💻 Visit the Heinemann Bookshop at www.heinemann.co.uk/library to browse our catalogue and order online.

Produced by Monkey Puzzle Media Ltd
Gissing's Farm, Fressingfield, Suffolk IP21 5SH, UK

First published in Great Britain by Heinemann Library, Halley Court, Jordan Hill, Oxford OX2 8EJ, part of Harcourt Education.
Heinemann is a registered trademark of Harcourt Education Ltd.

Author: Paul Mason
Editorial: Catherine Burch
Series Designer: Tim Mayer
Book Designer: Vicky Short
Illustrator: Sam Lloyd
Production: Séverine Ribierre

Originated by Repro Multi-Warna
Printed in Hong Kong, China by Wing King Tong

ISBN 0 431 17530 6
07 06 05 04 03
10 9 8 7 6 5 4 3 2 1

British Library Cataloguing in Publication Data
Mason, Paul
Diary of a Motocross Freak
796.7'56
A full catalogue record for this book is available from the British Library.

Acknowledgements
All photographs supplied by Red Eye Media Ltd (Gary Freeman), except: p. **15 top right** and **bottom left** by Red Eye Media Ltd (Kawasaki); p. **23** four exercise pictures by Paul Mason; p. **27 centre left**, **middle**, **centre right**, bottom by Red Eye Media Ltd (B.R. Nicholls).

Every effort has been made to contact copyright holders of any material reproduced in this book. Any omissions will be rectified in subsequent printings if notice is given to the publishers.

Attention!

This book is about motocross, which is a dangerous sport. This book is not an instruction manual or a substitute for proper lessons. Every year people are killed riding motocross – make sure you aren't one of them. Get expert instruction, always wear the right safety equipment, and make sure you ride within your own ability.

CONTENTS

For new motocross fans, MX words
are explained on page 30.

I AM A MOTOCROSS FREAK

Matt Slater Fact File:
Age: sixteen
Years riding: two
Favourite foods: pasta and cheese (in training), burgers and fries (not in training!)
Hobbies: riding motocross, computer games, listening to music

This is me!

I am Matt Slater. This is the story of how I got into riding motocross bikes. I've used pages from my diary to remember the best, most important moments in my riding career so far. The first day I ever got on a bike, for example, or learning to corner, getting a riding outfit, my first race — it's all here. One day, when I'm a world-famous rider, this stuff might be worth a lot of money.

Then again, it might not...

This is me with my current bike.

JUNE

	4	11	18	25
	5	12	19	26
	6	13	20	27
	7	14	21	28
1	8	15	22	29
2	9	16	23	30
3	10	17	(24)	

SUNDAY 24 JUNE
THE EARLY DAYS

The borrowed safety kit is a little bit big for me!

My first-ever day as a motocross rider! I finally persuaded Dad to pull the dust covers off the old 50cc bike in the garage. He filled it up with fuel, borrowed some safety kit for me, and we were ready! My friend Dan came with us and had a go too, and we both found it a bit tricky at first. The hardest thing was changing gear, using both hands and a foot at the same time.

We had a break for some lunch then tried again. This time it all seemed a lot easier. I managed to move the bike around in quite tight turns without overbalancing or stalling. By the end of the afternoon I could even ride over some of the rougher ground.

I'm hooked on motocross! I can't wait to go again and learn more.

6

CLUTCH LEVER — PULL THIS IN AT THE START TO PUT THE BIKE IN GEAR, THEN RELEASE IT AS YOU REV THE BIKE TO PULL AWAY

THROTTLE — TWIST TOWARDS YOURSELF TO ACCELERATE, AND AWAY TO SLOW DOWN

CHANGING GEAR:

Changing up: get the revs high and get your toe under the gear lever. Ease off the throttle and put upward pressure on the lever. As soon as the new gear engages, get back on the revs.

Changing down: same technique but come right off the throttle before shifting down.

BRAKE LEVER — CONTROLS THE FRONT BRAKE, WHICH IS THE MOST POWERFUL ONE

GEAR PEDAL — CLICKS DOWN ONCE INTO FIRST GEAR, THEN UP INTO SECOND, THIRD AND SO ON

BRAKE PEDAL — CONTROLS THE BACK BRAKE, NOT AS POWERFUL AS THE FRONT

AUGUST

	6	13	20	27
	7	14	21	28
1	8	15	22	29
2	9	16	23	30
3	10	17	24	31
4	11	18	25	
5	12	19	26	

We went to a specialist motocross shop – the salesman was really helpful. The best thing of all was that he actually told me to buy some things that were cheaper than the ones I'd been looking at! The more expensive stuff didn't fit as well, so it wouldn't have been as good in a crash.

FRIDAY 31 AUGUST
THE RIGHT GEAR

Went on a big shopping trip today to buy a full set of safety clothes and equipment. I'm wearing my new gear while writing the diary – it's important to break it in a bit before going out on a bike.

HELMET – most important bit of gear. Broken limbs mend, but a cracked head might be forever! Must fit snugly so that it won't move around in a crash, but not be so tight it gives me a headache.

GOGGLES – need to fit comfortably but snugly around your helmet and be sealed around the edges.

8

MX BOOTS – reinforced boots protect feet from being crushed.

GLOVES – need proper motocross (or MX) gloves, with protection for knuckles and special padding for the palms of your hands.

BODY ARMOUR – needs to meet safety standards for protection. I feel like a linebacker wearing this!

SHIRT – covers body armour and gives protection from weather and cold.

TROUSERS – these have to fit well and protect your legs from bumps and bashes, as well as the weather.

9

SEPTEMBER

	3	10	17	24
	4	11	18	25
	5	12	19	26
	6	13	20	27
	7	14	21	28
1	8	15	22	29
2	9	16	23	30

lovely mud!

SUNDAY 30 SEPTEMBER
ENDURO-TASTIC

Dan, my other friend John and I just got back from our first taste of enduro riding. Excellent fun! But I'm so tired I could hardly get the energy to open my diary.

Enduro is a bit like long-distance motocross. Instead of riding around a short circuit lots of times, you ride a longer route over lots of different types of ground. It's really hard work trying to handle the bike over tricky bumps, fallen branches and other obstacles. But battling through the stream was excellent, especially as John got soaked because he'd put his foot down in the water!

Me with some friends I met at enduro riding.

Kersplooosh!!

John's bike stopped when he soaked it in a stream. It was a good job there were three of us — I went for help while Dan stayed with John. Would have been even better to have a mobile phone with us!

Worst bit of the day was having to clean the bikes afterwards — if you don't do it they stop working properly, but all we really wanted to do was get in the car and go to sleep.

DAVE'S PAGE

Last year an old friend of my dad's who lives in the USA visited us. His son Dave is into bikes too, so we email each other.

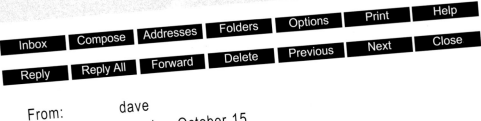

Inbox | Compose | Addresses | Folders | Options | Print | Help | Previous | Next | Close | Reply | Reply All | Forward | Delete

From: dave
Date: Monday, October 15
To: matt
Subject: pix, trails

>Hey, Matt, how's it going?

>Thought you'd like to see some of this stuff. We borrowed a digital camera and took a load of photos the other day. I've attached them to the email. I don't know how they'll come out, but they should give you an idea of what the trails are like around here.

>Pic one is just me with my bike. Pics two and three are from a local trail we call Route 68. It's a complete blast. I guess it's pretty different from the kind of trail you're used to riding in England. The weather's dry here most of the time, so by the end of summer the earth's baked rock hard. You have to use different techniques when you're riding in mud, and it's much easier to lose the front wheel and wash out. I use softer tire pressures for more grip, and set the suspension softer too.

>Signing off now - got school stuff to do!

>Dave

>PS Good luck with buying your new bike!

Smart bike!

MARCH

	4	11	18	25
	5	12	19	26
	6	13	20	27
	7	14	21	28
1	8	15	22	29
2	9	16	23	30
3	10	17	24	31

FRIDAY 22 MARCH
BIKE!

New bike! New bike, new bike, new bike! I've just gone with my dad to pick up my first-ever new bike. I've been sitting in the garage looking at it, but it's too cold so I had to come in.

When I still wanted to ride motocross after the winter I think my dad realized that it wasn't just a passing thing. He finally worked out that in the long run it might be cheaper to buy me a bike of my own than to keep renting them. I suppose it was good to rent first because it gave me a chance to check out loads of different bikes before we bought one. But it's great to have my own bike at last!

LOW ENOUGH SEAT TO BE ABLE TO TOUCH THE GROUND EASILY

HIGH MUDGUARD KEEPS DIRT OFF (IN THEORY!)

This model has been out for a couple of years — magazine review says no reliability problems, engine is solid.

125cc ENGINE LIGHT ENOUGH TO HANDLE EASILY AND HAS GOOD ACCELERATION

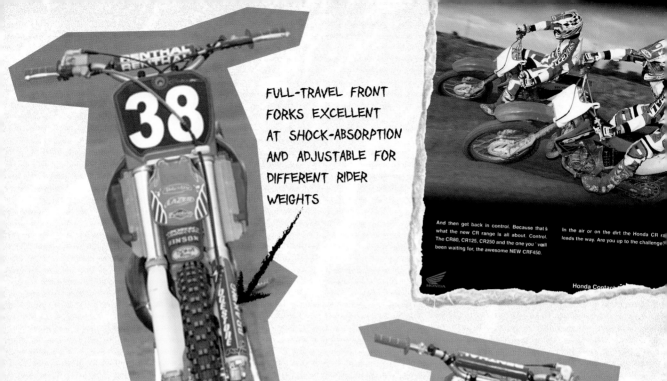

FULL-TRAVEL FRONT
FORKS EXCELLENT
AT SHOCK-ABSORPTION
AND ADJUSTABLE FOR
DIFFERENT RIDER
WEIGHTS

KNOBBLY TYRES GIVE
EXCELLENT GRIP

I got ideas from
magazines about
good bikes to buy.

FOOTPEGS AND
SEAT GIVE UPRIGHT
RIDING POSITION —
GOOD BALANCE AND
VIEW AHEAD

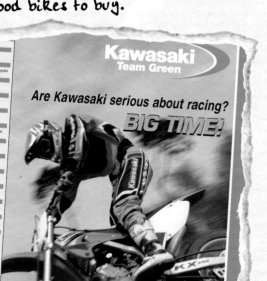

15

APRIL

1	8	15	22	29
2	9	16	23	30
3	10	17	24	
4	11	18	25	
5	12	19	26	
6	13	20	27	
7	14	21	28	

FRIDAY 5 APRIL — 11PM
NERVES

Having trouble getting to sleep tonight — I'm going on a motorcycle course tomorrow. It's organized by the place where I got my new bike, as a way of making sure everyone who buys a bike knows how to use it safely.

Dave sent me a checklist of things to run through before I get going and tips while I'm riding. I'm still worried everyone else will be a lot more experienced than me, though. Am I going to be the lapper at the back all the time?

DAVE'S TOP TIPS!

1 Listen to your instructors — they're way better riders than you.

2 Never go faster than you want just to keep up with other people.

3 Work on getting the techniques right first, then worry about going quickly. No one learns anything at full speed.

4 If you're worried you're going to crash, don't look at the thing you're afraid you might hit — your body (and the bike!) will follow your eyes and you will crash. Instead focus on the safe course you need to take — round the corner, or to the side of an obstacle. Trust yourself and the bike to get you there.

I think everything's ready: bike checked over (plenty of oil and fuel), clothes washed, boots cleaned up after last ride, helmet checked for damage. Everything's in the bag; now I can't wait to get there and get going.

Mum is not happy about all the extra washing!

APRIL

1	8	15	22	29
2	9	16	23	30
3	10	17	24	
4	11	18	25	
5	12	19	26	
6	13	20	27	
7	14	21	28	

Racing starts — keep weight forward on the bike and twist throttle about halfway back. Let clutch out fast but smooth, twisting throttle back to full power as you go. Get feet on pegs as soon as possible!

SATURDAY 6 APRIL
LEARNING TO BE GOOD

So tired after today, but it was fantastic! I think I learnt more in about six hours than I would have in six months of just riding with my friends. I've got some excellent photos, too.

The first day (today) was all about basic techniques for racing: body position on the bike, starting and accelerating, and slowing down. Tomorrow they're going to tell us about getting smoothly round corners and doing jumps. Can't wait!

Brakes — best only to brake going in a straight line, not during a turn. If you have to brake going round a corner, use back brake if possible.

18

Standing position — basic position for riding motocross bike fast. Standing on footpegs with knees slightly bent, keep arms bent too. Aim to feel balanced but slightly crouched forward.

Slowing down — use gears and engine to slow down smoothly. Pull in clutch and change to lower gear (e.g. third to second). Let clutch out but match revs to the speed you're going so bike doesn't do a big lurch. Then close throttle to slow down.

19

APRIL

1	8	15	22	29
2	9	16	23	30
3	10	17	24	
4	11	18	25	
5	12	19	26	
6	13	20	27	
7	14	21	28	

Me cornering fast! Inside foot down for balance, toes pointed forward so my feet could slide on the dirt.

SUNDAY 7 APRIL

This has been such a good course – and I'm not just saying that because I came second in the race at the end! I feel like I'm riding twice as fast, and much more safely as well. Being given tips by people who used to be professional racers is a really good way to make your riding better.

The first thing we covered today was smooth, fast cornering. The main thing I learned was that it's your speed as you come up to the bend that's important. If you have to brake late you lose loads of ground to other riders who are going round the corner more smoothly.

Airtime!

The jumps were scary. Moving your weight back while you're in the air makes the back wheel land first, and moving it forward drops the front wheel down. On most jumps you have to land with the back wheel.

Landing a tabletop, the only jump where you land on your front wheel.

If we had a bigger garden, and Mum wasn't so keen on roses, we could build a jump!

Where you see the two sides of the track meet as they go round a bend is called the vanishing point. If the vanishing point is coming towards you, you need to slow down. If it's moving away from you, gas it!

21

APRIL

1	8	15	22	29
2	9	16	23	30
3	10	17	24	
4	11	18	25	
5	12	19	26	
6	13	20	27	
7	14	21	28	

MONDAY 8 APRIL
THE NEXT CARMICHAEL

I have decided that I must be fitter. Only fitness will allow me to conquer the motocross world and become the next Ricky Carmichael! I might have won the race at the end of my course if I hadn't been so tired.

Dave has sent me some exercises he found on the Internet, which he says are great for warming up. Each stretch should be done ten times on each side. To get fitter I'm going to swim one day, run the next and then rest on the third day. For swimming I'm just going to swim at a steady speed – about 85 % of full speed for half an hour. For running, which I hate, I have a cunning plan to ease myself into it...

Carmichael wouldn't be able to do this if he didn't go running!

SHOULDER STRETCHES (DO BOTH SIDES)

WAIST STRETCH (ON BOTH SIDES)

THIGH STRETCHES (BOTH LEGS)

CALF STRETCH

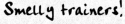

RUNNING - HALF AN HOUR EVERY OTHER DAY.

Week 1 - run for four minutes, rest for six; run for two minutes, rest for eight; run for four minutes, rest for six.

Week 2 - run for six minutes, rest for four; run for four minutes, rest for six; run for six minutes, rest for four.

Week 3 - run for twelve minutes, rest for eight; run for ten minutes.

Week 4 - run for 30 minutes.

Smelly trainers!

JUNE

3	10	17	24
4	11	18	25
5	12	19	26
6	13	20	27
7	14	21	28
1	8	15	22	29
2	9	16	23	30

SUNDAY 16 JUNE — 1.23 AM!
FIRST RACE

Just got home after my first race. We had to unload the bike and clean the trailer ready to go back to the rental place, so it's very late.

When we got there this morning I was really nervous. I went to confirm my entry with the race marshals, and wandered around watching the other racers. I thought they all looked a lot more professional than I did, and there were some really expensive bikes there.

I studied the course carefully, and I could see that if I got a slow start I might get held up at the first corner. The corner also looked tighter than it really was,

Early in the race

so you could go a little bit faster than you thought. When the race started I just nailed it, and got to the corner with the front group of riders. Most people seemed to slow down a lot for the corner, but I knew I could hold a bit more speed. I managed to sneak past a few more people in the bend.

After that I just tried to hang on, staying focused on the next section of the course. When I saw the finishing flag I had no idea where I'd come — I was third! The running must be paying off...

24

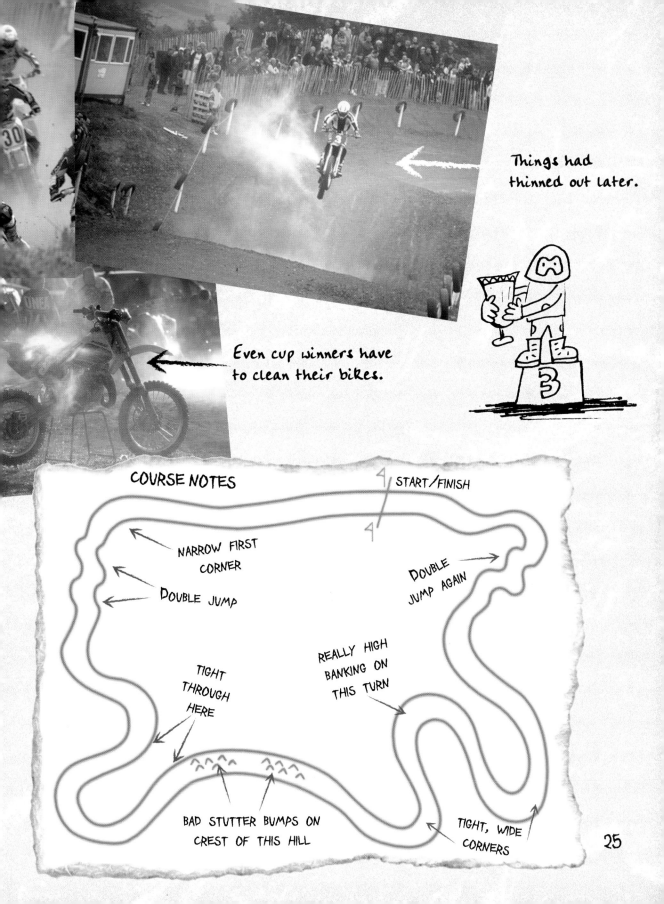

Things had thinned out later.

Even cup winners have to clean their bikes.

COURSE NOTES

START/FINISH

NARROW FIRST CORNER

DOUBLE JUMP

DOUBLE JUMP AGAIN

REALLY HIGH BANKING ON THIS TURN

TIGHT THROUGH HERE

BAD STUTTER BUMPS ON CREST OF THIS HILL

TIGHT, WIDE CORNERS

EMAIL HISTORY

Inbox	Compose	Addresses	Folders	Options	P
Reply	Reply All	Forward	Delete	Previous	

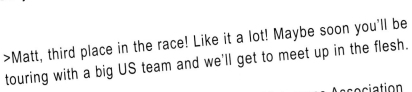

From: dave
Date: Saturday, July 13
To: matt
Subject: old timers

>Matt, third place in the race! Like it a lot! Maybe soon you'll be touring with a big US team and we'll get to meet up in the flesh.

>I got you some info from the American Motocross Association (AMA) website. The history section says that motocross actually started in Europe after the Second World War – us Americans were more interested in riding round flat dirt tracks. I find this amazing, considering how popular motocross and supercross are here now.

>MX spread to the US in the late 1960s and 1970s, when European stars regularly came over here and whipped us. But by the 1980s it was so popular here, and there were so many riders, that the US was on top of the MX heap. Now the AMA Supercross Series is the biggest dirt-bike event in the world by far.

>Best thing I found out on the site is how much money the riders make now. Even the hot sixteen-year-olds are making six figures a year. The big stars can earn a million dollars a year from their riding contracts, prize money and clothing sponsors.

>Info on the 125cc class of supercross events is attached, just in case you want to get into it somehow.

>Dave

Wheeee!

Supercross Format

2 heats, with a last-chance qualifier as well.

Heats 1 and 2:
20 riders race six laps.
The first nine go through to the final.

Last chance:
22 riders (the ones who did not get through heats 1 and 2) race four laps.
The first four go through.

Final race:
22 riders race fifteen laps.
The winner wins!

Dave's info on supercross events

Supercross at night looks exciting!

Cool old photos. Back in the early days MX was called 'rough riding'!

HEROES

1. Ricky Carmichael
Ricky was only 22 when he won the 2002 AMA 250cc Supercross title with 356 points and eleven race wins. By the end of the 2002 series, Carmichael had won 24 supercross races in the last two seasons. He's not likely to slow down in the near future.

2. David Vuillemin
Carmichael's nearest rival finished the 2002 AMA season with 301 points but just three wins. Always chasing Carmichael, he looks like one of the few riders who might be able to beat him one day.

3. Jeremy McGrath
McGrath struggled in 2002, but by then he'd already won the AMA 250cc Supercross title seven times! Between 1993 and 2000 he lost the title only once, in 1997.

4. Stefy Bau

Winner of the Women's AMA 125cc World Cup in 1999, Bau comes from Milan in Italy but races in the USA. Her first year was spent riding in 'B' class races against amateur riders. She says that on the 'amateur side guys don't like to be beaten by a woman' and that year was 'really hard'. Stefy made it through to become a professional rider.

5. Team Motul Yamaha

A small semi-pro Australian team with an all-female lineup. Most of the members started their motocross careers racing against men, because there were no women's races at the time. Women's MX scene is now growing fast in Australia.

David Vuillemin and
Jeremy McGrath

MX WORDS FOR BEGINNERS

Berm
Build-up of dirt on the outer edge of a turn. Acts as banking to help the riders get round faster.

Casing it
Not jumping quite far enough on a double or triple (see below), and landing on the top of the jump instead of the down-slope. Often results in landing on the engine casings, hence 'casing it'.

Doubles/triples
Jumps made up of more than one mound of earth, allowing riders to jump up the first one and land on the down-slope of the second or third. Triples are most common in supercross.

Endo
Go head-first over the handlebars.

Holeshot
The position of the first rider through the first turn of the race.

Lapper
A slow rider who ends up being lapped by those in front.

Line
The path a bike takes along the track or round a turn. People might talk about a 'fast line' or a 'smooth line'.

Motocross (MX)
Outdoor motorbike races through natural obstacles such as hills and woods. The courses are generally longer than supercross (see below) and the jumps and other obstacles are less radical.

On the pipe
When a rider's going very fast someone might say he or she is 'on the pipe'. Bike exhaust pipes work best at certain engine speeds, and when a rider is really going fast they're riding the bike at its best, hence 'on the pipe'.

Supercross
A series of races in the USA that take place inside huge stadiums and domes that are normally home to NFL American Football or major league baseball teams. The one- or two-mile tracks are built using up to 700 tonnes of dirt, shaped into obstacles from which the riders launch up to fifteen metres into the air.

Wash out
When the front wheel loses grip and slides away from the line (see above). Washing out usually ends in a crash.

INTERNET LINKS

www.amaproracing.com
The Internet site of American Motocross Association.

www.media.suzuki.com
Interesting section on the history of MX, plus general information about the sport.

www.motocross.com.au
Australia's leading MX website.

www.motocross.com
This is an on-line magazine with all kinds of MX-related things listed, plus links to other MX sites.

www.mxlarge.com
Magazine site with links to the current race results and positions in the AMA Motocross and Supercross races.

BOOKS AND MAGAZINES

Radical Sports: Motocross by Gary Freeman (Heinemann Library, 2002).

To The Limit: Motocross by Gary Freeman (Hodder Wayland, 2000).

Dirtbike British magazine that covers European bike reviews, rider profiles, news of competitions and other special features.

Transworld Motocross An American magazine with similar content to 'Dirtbike', but focussing on the American riding scene.

FILM AND VIDEO

'On Any Sunday' Classic movie made by Bruce Brown, who also made the famous surfing movie 'Endless Summer'. The movie was backed by the film star Steve McQueen, who was famous for riding a motorcycle in the war film 'The Great Escape'.

INDEX